Reviews on the author's
Become a National Board Certified Teacher?"

"I found this book to be very helpful and sound. For the 'newbies', I highly recommend investing in this book! Jerry is extremely knowledgeable and he helped me through the process..."
—Eleanor Joyce, NBCT, Virginia

"Thank you for simplifying the process for us! The book has helped me tremendously in organizing my thoughts. Thanks for the impact you've made..."
—Karuna Chettri, Montessori Primary Teacher, Maryland

"Thank the Lord I found this book! I finally made it! This was my third attempt. I bought Jerry Parks' book, and took the advice. I passed with a 3** total score, and I made a 4.0 on my retake entry. I addressed every instructional component, remaining mindful that how I answered each question should reflect linkage with the standards. I thank the Lord that I found this book, and that I bought it! I wished that I would've had it 3 years ago. Thanks so much from a Louisiana Lady!"
—Laura in Louisiana

"Having the pleasure of working with Jerry Parks is one of the many highlights of my job, and to read and share his writing has enlightened so many other professionals. This little book possesses a vast amount of pertinent information that promotes completion of certification in a timely and efficient manner. The "tips" are precise, and written in a manner easily understandable and adaptable. For candidates seriously pursuing National Board Certification, this book is a must read."
—Billie Travis. Kentucky "Teacher of the Year", 2005

Mentoring the NBPTS Candidate: A Facilitator's Guide

Other works by Jerry Parks:

"So, You Want to Become a National Board Certified Teacher?"—a handbook of tips, suggestions, and resources for new *NBPTS* candidates.

"Teacher Under Construction: Things I Wish I'd Known"—a handbook to help new middle school teachers in their first year of teaching.

"With Joseph in the University of Adversity: The Mizraim Principles"—principles for successful living, based on the life of Joseph the Hebrew in the Old Testament.

"Dragons, Grasshoppers & Frogs!"—a simplified commentary for teenagers on the Book of Revelation.

Mentoring the NBPTS Candidate: A Facilitator's Guide

A Mentor's Handbook for Successfully Coaching the NBPTS Candidate Through the Certification Process

Jerry L. Parks, Ed.S., NBCT

Weekly Reader Press
New York Lincoln Shanghai

Mentoring the NBPTS Candidate: A Facilitator's Guide
A Mentor's Handbook for Successfully Coaching the NBPTS Candidate Through the Certification Process

Copyright © 2006 by Jerry Parks

All rights reserved. No part of this book may be used or reproduced by any means, graphic, electronic, or mechanical, including photocopying, recording, taping or by any information storage retrieval system without the written permission of the publisher except in the case of brief quotations embodied in critical articles and reviews.

Weekly Reader Press
an imprint of iUniverse, Inc.
and the Weekly Reader Corporation

iUniverse books may be ordered through booksellers or by contacting:

iUniverse
2021 Pine Lake Road, Suite 100
Lincoln, NE 68512
www.iuniverse.com
1-800-Authors (1-800-288-4677)

ISBN-13: 978-0-595-40483-4
ISBN-10: 0-595-40483-9

Printed in the United States of America

Contents

Preface xi

Chapter 1:   You as Mentor:
Beginning with your Candidate 1
(Mentor Quiz, Core Propositions)

Chapter 2:   Accomplished Teaching:
the Model & the Goal 7
(Practicing Accomplished Teaching)

Chapter 3:   You'll be Working with Adults:
How they Learn 11
(They are different from your students)

Chapter 4:   Setting Up Your Mentorship:
Ethics, Forms & Inquiry...................................15
(The Ten Commandments of Mentoring; Asking the right questions; Resources; Sample forms)

Chapter 5:   Knowledge of Students:
the Core of Your Candidates' Content 27
(The students, the classroom & the lesson)

Chapter 6:   The Writing Process:
Fabric of Your Candidate's Success 31
(Recognizing and practicing effective writing)

Chapter 7: Evidence, Scoring & Assessment:
Student Learning & the Standards 36
(Helping your candidate know what the assessors will be looking for)

Chapter 8: Tips & Reflections on Entries 1-4 40
(Carefully examining every aspect of your candidate's portfolio; Sample forms)

Chapter 9: Mentoring the Advanced Candidate:
Achieving Success the Next time Through 54
(Special Considerations)

Chapter 10: Packing the Box & the Assessment Center:
Final Considerations 57
(Tying up all the loose ends)

Bibliography and References 61

About the Author 63

Author acknowledgements

I would like to offer a special thanks to Lynn Hines, long-time director of the Kentucky *NBPTS* Program, with whom I had the honor to work as Kentucky *NBPTS* Regional Coordinator. Her tireless work made our program one of the finest in the nation

I would also like to thank Carole Mullins, Marsha Reddick, and all my Regional Coordinator cohorts for their work as mentor trainers in the Kentucky *NBPTS* program, and Eleanor Joyce for her helpful suggestions in making this book possible. Finally, I would like to express appreciation to Yvonne Woodward, whose work with advanced candidates, and suggestions regarding the same were especially valuable.

Preface

A mentor is defined as one who gives of one's self to guide and train another toward excellence. This book is designed to lend support to the mentors of *NBPTS* candidates across America who are giving their time—often without-remuneration—to help members of their profession excel. The work is the compilation of suggestions, not only from the author, but also from countless other *NBPTS* mentors with whom I have worked, and from excellent mentor-training programs, which I have been fortunate to participate in.

Mentoring is a daunting process and an important responsibility. Mentoring the *NBPTS* candidate is especially so.

Mentors should have completed the *NBPTS* process themselves. Board certification is achieved through testing, submission of a portfolio comprised of videotapes of the candidate's teaching and student interaction, analyzed student writing samples, and teacher artifacts reflecting documented accomplishments.

While there are many well-organized state *NBPTS* mentoring programs, many who seek to mentor candidates must undertake this endeavor unsupported. It is the author's hope that such mentors will find this book especially useful.

There is obviously not one right way to gain *NBPTS* certification. Neither is there one right way to mentor. However, utilizing tips, helps, and suggested activities from those who have completed an organized mentor-training process can greatly assist those who seek to mentor others. Mentors should remember, however, that the *NBPTS* does set forth certain ethical standards for mentoring. These, as well as other generally accepted mentoring standards are clearly substantiated throughout this book.

Much of the material presented in this book is similar to material presented in the author's work for candidates: *"So, You Want to Become a National Board*

Certified Teacher?". It is strongly suggested that candidates being mentored have access to that work due to additional material and information. While there is some necessary overlap between the two books, the author has attempted to avoid redundancy as much as possible.

All information presented was current as of the publication date, and may be subject to change. More detailed information regarding the mentoring process is available from http://www.*NBPTS*.org/, and this book is in no way connected with the *National Board for Professional Teaching Standards* or its affiliates. It represents solely the opinions of the author.

Chapter 1

"You as Mentor: Beginning with your Candidate"

(Mentor Quiz, Core Propositions)

Introduction

Welcome to mentoring your *NBPTS* candidate! Whether this is your first *NBPTS* mentoring experience, or you are already a veteran mentor, this book is designed to offer you as many valuable helps as possible. However, because some states have their own organized *NBPTS* mentoring structure, some of the material contained in this book may have to be amended or modified. In addition, the way you use this book may somewhat depend on whether you are mentoring your candidates individually, or in a group (cohort) setting. Nevertheless, even with modifications, the suggested activities, tips, checklists, and resources should prove helpful.

While there are no hard and fast rules for mentorship, there are some basic guidelines you would do well to observe. If you are not a part of a state-regulated *NBPTS* mentoring program, answer the FAQ's below to see how you score with some generally accepted mentor 'do's and don'ts'. (Answers appear on the Bibliography & References page at the end of this book.)

1. As mentor, am I required to read my candidate's entries and watch their videos at least one time?

2. If my candidate does not certify the first year, are they required by the *NBPTS* to begin the entire process over again?

3. Is it true that the primary reason candidates generally score low on the Documented Accomplishments Entry is because they do not connect the listed activities to student learning?

4. If my candidate chooses to retake as many as 6-7 entries, might I advise them that it could be more cost effective for them to start the entire portfolio over?

5. As mentor, would it be OK to work with my candidate through email at times, rather than in person, if we are both OK with that arrangement?

6. If my candidate is having trouble during the certification process, is it permissible to share this with their colleagues so they can lend support?

7. If my candidate starts the portfolio over, will they have another three attempts to complete it successfully?

8. Is it true that assessors are trained to find what is wrong in the candidate's writing, and how the writing fails to meet the *NBPTS* Standards?

9. As mentor, is it a good mentoring policy to allow my candidate to view my completed portfolio in order to give them a mental picture of what one should look like?

10. If my candidate narrows down several activities to use for the video entries, should I, as mentor, advise them on which one will likely score the highest?

11. As mentor, should I help my candidate with the basics such as spelling, grammar, and sentence structure?

12. Is there really one right way to write a 'winning entry' for *NBPTS*?

13. My candidate has asked to look at a portion of the video entry from my personal portfolio. Should I let them?

14. As mentor, if I am working with several candidates at the same time, is it permissible to allow candidates to read each others' entries?

15. As mentor, may I share with my candidate an excerpt from a writing entry from my personal portfolio as long as I don't share any completed entry?

16. Is my main job as mentor to help my candidate become self-directed, rather than to supply information to them?

17. As mentor, would it be OK to help my candidate understand the scoring process by assigning my 'opinioned' scores to an entry?

18. To help my candidate prepare, could I share a question I recall from the Assessment Center just to give them an idea what to expect?

19. All questions should be directed to 1-800-22TEACH.

20. Is my mentor/candidate relationship much like a teacher/student relationship?

21. If my candidate cites any research in their entries, are they required to include a bibliography?

22. Is it true that even though my candidate is an adult professional, he/she will often lack self-confidence when going through this process?

23. Is it true that spelling, grammar, and punctuation determine a part of the portfolio score?

24. Are the Assessment Center exercises content-based like the writing entries?

25. What if two candidates submit nearly identical portfolios, should the candidates assume this infraction would most likely be caught?

26. I have heard that it is generally advisable for mentors to work with candidates who are *not* pursuing the same certification area, in order to give a different perspective. Is this true?

27. Should the first meeting with my candidate involve mutual expectations, a syllabus, and a timeline?

28. I want to include snacks and beverages at my meetings with my candidate, but was told these are distractions, and are inappropriate. Is this true?

29. My candidate was told that humor, teacher mistakes, and student misunderstandings have no place in the final submitted videos. Is that true?

30. Am I correct in telling my candidate that if he/she retakes an entry, the higher of the two scores will count toward certification?

NBPTS Core Propositions

If you are mentoring, you are most likely already board certified, and the Core Propositions of the *NBPTS* will be readily familiar to you. Just for the record however, they are:

Proposition 1: *Commitment to Students*
Teachers should believe that all students can learn, regardless of background, and tailor instruction toward holistic learning by addressing multiple intelligences.

Proposition 2: *Knowledge of Subject*
Students must be challenged by teachers who know them holistically, understand their teaching subject matter fully, and are able to generate multiple paths toward learning.

Proposition 3: *Management of Behavior*
Teachers must grow professionally, and understand how to manage, motivate, monitor, and assess students through appropriate activities, and acceptable learning goals.

Proposition 4: *Professional Growth*
Teachers must make appropriate choices, interact with—and learn from—colleagues, and continually seek ways to gain more knowledge in their subject area.

Proposition 5: *Community Learning*
Teachers should collaborate with other professionals, parents, and their community in addressing the holistic needs of their students.

Suggested activity

As you begin your mentorship, have your candidate define and explain:

- ✓ *What each of these propositions mean*
- ✓ *Why each proposition is important*
- ✓ *Which proposition they feel they are the strongest/weakest in addressing, and why*
- ✓ *How they address, or might address, each of the propositions*

Helping your candidate decide on their certification area

If your candidate has not chosen the area in which they will pursue certification, discuss the following considerations with them.

- They should visit the *NBPTS* website to check current certification areas.
- They should be teaching in the subject area specified by the certification.
- They should determine which standards and certification area best exemplifies the subject they currently teach.
- They should consider if they have the educational training and experience which will allow them to pursue work in that area of certification.
- A minimum of 51% of the students they teach must be in the age-range specified.

Common threads through all certification areas

No matter which certification area your candidate is pursuing, there are common threads which run through each:

- ➢ The three types of writing (see Chapter 6)
- ➢ Knowing and using the *NBPTS* Standards in each certification area (see Chapter 7)
- ➢ Emphasizing continual, two-way communication with parents, students, and students with each other
- ➢ Demonstrating knowledge of how students development, and how to set realistic, age-appropriate, and measurable goals for them (see Chapter 5)
- ➢ Creating lessons based on student and curricular needs

➤ Documented Accomplishments (see Chapter 8)

Suggested activity

To get your candidate started in the process, have them list and discuss how they emphasize two-way communication with parents on a regular basis.

Chapter 2

"Accomplished Teaching: the Model & the Goal!"

(Practicing Accomplished Teaching)

Your candidates may or may not be an accomplished teacher. Nevertheless, accomplished teaching is the goal for your candidate as well as the standard of excellence by which he/she will be evaluated. Understanding this, let's see what an accomplished teacher does. In this way, you can encourage your candidate to identify, model, and feature accomplished teaching throughout his/her entry writing. The following descriptors are taken from the excellent work: *"Enhanced Architecture of Accomplished Teaching"* (Einhorn, 2002).

- Accomplished teachers know their students, what their students need, and when their students need it.

- Accomplished teachers know how to set high, yet reachable goals for their students, at the right time, and in the right setting.

- Accomplished teachers know how to implement instruction designed to attain such goals.

- Accomplished teachers know how and when to evaluate their students in light of these goals.

- Accomplished teachers know how to provide meaningful and timely feedback to students regarding their level of accomplishment of these goals.

- Accomplished teachers know how to reflect on student learning, and the effectiveness of instructional design.

- Accomplished teachers know how to evaluate what has and has not worked, and reset worthwhile goals for student achievement.

- Accomplished teachers strive to excel above and beyond the normal expectations for every teacher, and make a conscious and deliberate effort to improve teaching and learning for themselves, and for their students.

Suggested activity

Have your candidate try to recall one or two of their own teachers whom they would consider an 'accomplished teacher'. Discuss with the candidate what personal and professional qualities made them choose these teachers. Next, have them list 5 things in their own professional life, which might evidence them as an 'accomplished teacher'. Finally, have them give several examples of how they meet the last characteristic of an 'accomplished teacher'.

To ensure that your candidates are modeling accomplished teaching, it might be helpful to have them evaluate their teaching methodology through a self-analysis. This could be done a number of times throughout your mentorship with them.

Suggested activity

If your candidate is having difficulty grasping the concept of what an accomplished/effective teacher looks like, suggest they watch 'Dead Poet's Society', or 'School of Life'. While these films in no way represent perfect teaching paradigms, they do show characteristics of highly effective teaching. Suggest that your candidate jot down some of these characteristics.

Suggested activity

Have candidates rate themselves on a scale you may wish to design. In this way, you can help them discover what improvements are needed, both for the classroom and for NBPTS assessment criteria.

- I know and recognize the abilities, interests, aspirations, and values, of most of my students.

- I know the subject matter and curriculum well enough to make sound decisions about what is important for my students to learn within, and across the curriculum.

- I design my classroom to be a creative, stimulating, and 'safe' environment, where students are comfortable taking intellectual risks, practicing democracy, and working collaboratively and independently.

- I make a conscious effort through design and modeling to help my students respect and appreciate individual and group differences.

- I create, select, and assess a varied and age-appropriate collection of materials, as well as utilize staff and community resources, in order to supplement my teaching and support learning.

- I engage my students in learning within and across all disciplines to help them understand how the subjects they study can be utilized to explore important issues in their lives and in the world around them.

- I understand that for each of my students there are multiple paths to learning the concepts of every school subject, and building overall understanding.

- I understand the strengths and weaknesses of various assessment methods, base my instruction around ongoing assessment, and encourage my students to monitor their own learning.

- I regularly initiate positive, interactive relationships with my students' families, and recognize them as an integral part of their child's education.

o   I continually analyze, evaluate, reflect on, and 'fine tune' the effectiveness of my teaching, and work with colleagues to help them improve their practice as well.

(Adapted from the *NBPTS Standards for Accomplished Middle Childhood/Generalist Teachers*)

Chapter 3

"You'll be Working with Adults: How they Learn"

(They are different from your students)

Your candidates will enter the certification process with apprehension (since they are not sure what to expect), motivation (since they have paid for this opportunity), and a great deal of confidence in you (since they assume you have all the answers!). It is important to remember however, that they are adults—not students—and to mentor them effectively, you must understand how adults learn differently. Compared to children and teens, adults have special needs and requirements as learners. The following considerations are adapted from *"Principles of Adult Learning",* by Stephen Lieb, writer for the Arizona Department of Health Services. As you work with your candidate, remember that:

- Adults are more self-directed—therefore you must allow them to be fully involved in the *NBPTS* certification process.

  As mentor, remember—Understand your candidate's perspective on things throughout your mentorship. Your candidate brings with them set habits and strong tastes. Remember, you are their facilitator, coach, and cheerleader—not their teacher. You must allow them to make choices, take responsibility for final decisions regarding their portfolio, and motivate them to be self-directed in their endeavors. Suggest often; tell sparingly. Build options within your plans.

- Adults bring a lifetime of personal experience and knowledge into the *NBPTS* certification process, yet often lack confidence in their abilities to learn new things that may intimidate them.

***As mentor, remember**—You must validate and affirm your candidate's prior knowledge, education, attitudes, prejudices, contributions, and values as you mentor them, and recognize that all these influence their decision-making. Integrate new ideas with existing knowledge. Channel the resources your candidates bring to you, and plan activities accordingly. Let them know the certification process is difficult but achievable. Allow them to share experiences. Be tactful in your correction and sincere in your encouragement.*

- Adults are more goal, and application-oriented in their tasks.

    ***As mentor, remember**—You must clearly organize and define what steps your candidates must take to achieve their goal of NBPTS certification. Success—not merely enjoying the process—is the goal. Help them to see that NBPTS certification validates personal advancement and professional achievement, and involves much more than mere monetary gain.*

- Adults are relevancy-oriented. That is, unlike children, they need to see the reason for doing something, and will respond most positively to suggestions that are interesting and meaningful.

    ***As mentor, remember**—It is important that you clarify why your candidate should, or should not do something in the teaching/writing process. Help them to understand why they are doing what you ask them to do, and how new information will be relevant to them.*

- Adults are practical and problem-centered. That is, they tend to focus on what is most useful to them in their work.

    ***As mentor, remember**—You must help your candidate see how your suggestions will be helpful to them as teacher, and as candidate. Consider the value of your candidate's time, and provide overviews, summaries, and examples to expedite the meetings. Adults respond better to showing than to telling.*

- Adults need respect. Remember to treat your candidates as equals in experience and knowledge, and allow them to voice opinions freely.

As mentor, remember—Don't 'talk down' to your candidate, and be careful in your choice of words which might evoke negative perceptions. As mentor, you are cheerleader and facilitator. You are in no way superior simply because you are an NBCT. Invite feedback on your mentorship, and allow your candidates to take ownership in your mentoring sessions. Above all, genuinely listen, and allow them to 'vent' when necessary.

- Adults have more preoccupations surrounding a central focus. While passing their *NBPTS* certification is a primary goal for your candidate, it is not the only important concern in his/her life.

As mentor, remember—You must plan your mentor sessions to make best use of your candidates' time. Let such planning be a joint endeavor. Allow for unforeseen changes throughout your mentoring process. Recognize that other responsibilities are equally important to your mentees, and reserve some time to listen to those. Be flexible in your scheduling.

- Adults recognize, and respond well, to authentic positive reinforcement and self-esteem building.

As mentor, remember—Praise genuinely—not artificially. Celebrate your candidate's effort as well as their achievement, but only in a sincere manner. Recognize incremental successes. Promote positive self-esteem through providing low-risk activities. Remember, your candidate trusts you to be a critical colleague offering honest feedback.

- Adults like their creature comforts, and learn best in a social, flexible, and comfortable environment.

As mentor, remember—In deciding on your mentoring environment, consider the furniture, refreshments, and other applicable amenities. Provide for introductory time, breaks, snacks, coffee, etc. Consider meeting in groups if you have several candidates.

Suggested activity

In your early sessions, establish a casual, low-key atmosphere. Inquire often regarding your candidate's family, recreational, and teaching environment. Take a genuine interest in aspects of his/her life apart from the NBPTS. Always be encouraging by saying 'when you certify', not 'if you certify'.

Chapter 4

"Setting Up Your Mentorship: Ethics, Forms & Inquiry"

(The Ten Commandments of Mentoring; Asking the right questions; Resources; Sample forms)

Your job as mentor is to focus your candidate's attention on his/her knowledge of students and subject, performance as teacher in the classroom, and growth as a professional educator. It is also your job to make sure they evidence these to the *NBPTS* through their submission of student work and knowledge, videotapes of classroom interaction, and written commentaries.

What should go without saying is that you must conduct your job as mentor in a professional and above-board manner at all times, and follow every guideline of the *NBPTS*. Because your work with your candidate is usually unmonitored, it is extremely important that you exhibit a professional ethic in every instruction you give to your candidate. Below is a generally accepted list of proper ethical conduct, and will help you stay on track. (For more specificity, check with the *NBPTS Guidelines for Ethical Candidate Support*.)

The Ethics of Mentoring

- ➢ Mentors must always protect the dignity and integrity of the *NBPTS* in everything they say and do.
- ➢ Mentors must stress confidentiality above all else with their candidate.
- ➢ Mentors must only share what can be publicly released.
- ➢ Mentors must direct candidates back to *NBPTS* Standards as the final authority on subject content questions.

- ➤ Mentors should not share personal, completed portfolios with candidates.
- ➤ Mentors must not share personal, completed videos with candidates.
- ➤ Mentors must not edit, revise, or rewrite candidate entries.
- ➤ Mentors must not score or make subjective qualitative judgments on candidate entries.
- ➤ Mentors must never discuss or disclose Assessment Center prompts.
- ➤ Mentors must not coach, or point out specific content to be studied, regarding the Assessment Center prompts.
- ➤ Mentors must not share negative opinions of a candidate with others.
- ➤ Mentors should report occasions of misconduct to 1-800-779-3339.

The Tools of Mentoring

The tools of mentoring are those things that will best promote a satisfactory and meaningful relationship between you and your candidate. Four of these are suggested by Costa & Garmston *(Cognitive Coaching, 1994)*. These include:

- *Trust*—trust is achieved through keeping confidentiality with your candidate. Trust is also nurtured through being consistent in how you deal with suggestions, criticisms, meetings, etc. You will also inspire trust through showing genuine interest in your candidate's success, and by being non-judgmental in dealing with your candidate's decision-making.

- *Rapport*—rapport is created through the language you use with your candidate, as well as the tone you use in speaking it. Candidates will learn much from your posture and body language, and facial expressions.

- *Effective Questioning*—questioning is the most important aspect in helping your candidate become self-directed in the completion their portfolio. Utilize probing, stimulating questions which help your candidate come to his/her own conclusions. (For example: "You know student learning took place, how?", or "How will this show your professional growth?", or "How did you feel this lesson went?")

- *Non-Judgmental Responses*—respond to your candidate's inquiries with pauses, paraphrasing, and redirection, *e.g.,* "I'm hearing you say…", or "Do I understand you to mean…?" (See Chapter 4)

The Characteristics of Mentoring

Robert Bacal, in *"The Role of The Facilitator—Understanding What Facilitators Really DO!"* furnishes a concise list of facilitator characteristics, and provides some traits which a good mentor should exhibit. An effective mentor:

- asks rather than tells
- pays personal compliments
- asks for other's opinions rather than always having to offer their own
- negotiates, rather than dictates, decision-making
- listens without interrupting
- is more enthusiastic than systematic
- is more outgoing than serious
- is more like a coach than a scientist
- can keep the big picture in mind while working on the nitty-gritty
- uses time intentionally
- affirms the wisdom of the client
- adapts to changing situations
- demonstrates professionalism & integrity
- demonstrates self-confidence and authenticity

The Forms you will need in Mentoring

Depending on whether or not you are mentoring as a part of an organized state program, you may or may not be required to keep and document certain forms. However, even if you are mentoring on your own, you would do well to create several types of forms in order to establish without ambiguity what will and will not transpire between you and your candidate, and when it will take place. Such forms will help you avoid numerous possible misunderstandings throughout your mentoring process, and will clarify expectations and schedules for both you and your candidate. Many of these forms can (and should) be joint compositions between you and your candidate. Suggested forms include a:

<u>*Candidate Contact form*</u>—which includes the candidate's:

- name
- candidacy area

- address
- phone and cell number
- email address
- school
- school email and phone
- best times to talk

Syllabus—which specifies:

- How many meetings you will have with your candidate
- The dates and times of each meeting
- How long each meeting will be
- Where the meetings will take place
- If the meetings will be in groups or individualized
- The topics of each meeting
- How you can be contacted in case of a change in plans

Each candidate should receive, sign, and date a copy of this syllabus. The syllabus can be amended throughout the process. (This syllabus might also include a writing draft timeline to keep you and your candidate on the same schedule.)

The most important aspect of your syllabus is the topic of each meeting. Topics which you may want to discuss at your meetings might include:

- An organizational 'get together' meeting
- Planning the year to best suit teaching the students and completing the process
- Examining, interpreting, and utilizing the standards
- The distinction between the 3 types of *NBPTS* portfolio writing
- Activities which will best feature your candidate as an accomplished teacher
- *NBPTS* ethics and the importance of confidentiality
- How to choose students and classes for writing entries
- How to use the computer and video camera most effectively
- Gathering artifacts for Documented Accomplishments
- Organizing the materials, entries, forms, candidate's work area, etc.
- The mechanics and pitfalls of taping
- The importance of making copies of all writing and tapes

- How to turn tapes into written analysis
- Mid-mentoring Q & A session (pause to refresh)
- Using the language of the standards in the writing process
- What constitutes clear, consistent, convincing evidence?
- Outside resources, and how to access them
- Incorporating Bloom's taxonomy and Gardner's Multiple Intelligences
- How to vary assessments and incorporate them into the teaching
- Preparing for, and understanding the Assessment Center
- Preparing, checking, packing and mailing the 'box'
- Using Verification Forms and creating communication logs
- Practicing Level 4 writing and how entries will be scored

<u>Meeting Sign-in Form</u>—which records the place, date, and time of each meeting. This will remove any doubt regarding attendance at your meetings with your candidate.

<u>Mentor Recording Sheet</u>—to keep records of all emails and phone calls, as well as what entries you read and what feedback you provided.

<u>Candidate/Mentor Expectation Agreement</u>—this may be completed before or during your first meeting with your candidate, and should clearly point out what you will and won't do as mentor, as well as what the candidate expects from you. (These expectations can be reconciled into a final agreement.) This helps to avoid misunderstandings and hurt feelings later. (Encourage your candidate to re-examine this form at regular intervals, and to let you know if they feel things are not going well. You should do the same for your candidate.) Possible areas on which you and your candidate can come to consensus:

- ❏ What is the mentor's role?
- ❏ Will you be reimbursed for mentoring?
- ❏ Discussion of ethics (what you cannot do)
- ❏ Discussion of *NBPTS* guidelines
- ❏ Will you read portfolio entries?
- ❏ Which portfolio entries will you read?
- ❏ How many readings will you provide?
- ❏ Will you read the same entry more than once?
- ❏ At what stage in the writing process will you read entries?

- ❏ Will you read entries sent by email?
- ❏ Will you review videos and student work? How many times?
- ❏ How long will you need in order to provide feedback?
- ❏ Will you provide outside resources and supplementary material?
- ❏ Will you provide feedback by email? If so, how soon/often will you respond?
- ❏ How much total mentoring time will you furnish your candidate? (Does this time include email correspondences?)
- ❏ How will you handle being unable to attend meetings?
- ❏ Will the candidate supply you with standards & guidelines for their area?

At the very least your candidate should agree to (among other things):

- Commit to the schedule and participate in the activities
- Share their fears, concerns and issues
- Maintain the confidentiality of the relationship
- Listen non-judgmentally and ask follow-up questions to clarify
- Fully understand the ethics and *NBPTS* Standards
- Take final responsibility for all aspects of their portfolio

(See sample agreement courtesy of Eleanor Joyce, *NBCT*, at the end of this chapter.)

Mentor Evaluation Sheet—whether or not you want a record of your candidate's evaluation is totally up to you. Generally, these are quite helpful to your future mentoring endeavors. Candidates will usually put on paper what they won't tell you face to face.

Be sure you and your candidate sign and date all forms. While these are not legal documents, they do serve as a tangible agreement should any disputes arise.

The Questioning Techniques of Mentoring

The finest questioning exposes the logic of someone else's thought. Since the days of Socrates, questioning techniques have been used to help learners reach their own conclusions. As mentor, your job is to do just that—help your candidate come to their own conclusions through eliciting and probing questioning—not by just supplying answers. Socratic questioning is only effective, however, if you, as mentor, really listen to what your candidate tells you.

In order to help your candidate analyze, evaluate, and conclude, consider using some of the following questioning techniques adapted from Richard Paul, in *"Critical Thinking: How to Prepare Students for a Rapidly Changing World"* (1993), during the mentoring sessions:

Questions in order to Clarify

"What do you mean by?"
"Could you give me an example?"
"How does this relate to community involvement?"
"Could you rephrase this another way?"
"Did you mean to imply...?"
"How might you elaborate?"

Questions in order to Assess

"How do you feel it went?"
"What made you feel that way?"
"What do you recall?"
"How can you improve on this next time?"
"What were you thinking when...?"
"What do you see as...?"
"What did her response tell you?"
"How does this evidence student learning?"

Questions to in order to Probe

"What are you intending through that?"
"Do I understand you to mean?"
"How might you justify this?"
"What might be an indicator?"
"Were you aware that...?"
"How can you be sure of this?"
"What is your evidence for this?"

Questions about Perspective

"How might someone else respond?"
"How might you answer that objection?"
"How might an assessor perceive that?"
"What might someone who disagrees say?"
"How might a non-educator see that?"

Questions about Implications

"What might be an alternative?"
"If you did, what might happen?"
"What else could result from this?"
"What effect might this have?"
"If this happened again what would you do?"

As you work with your candidate, remember—mentoring is an art, not a science. There is no one way to mentor correctly. However, there are numerous ways you might mentor incorrectly. In addition to the ethical and professional standards already discussed, let's review some following guidelines for successful mentoring:

The Ten Commandments of Mentoring

I. Thou shalt not give incorrect information to thy candidate. Research and know before you instruct. Don't be afraid to say, "I don't know."

II. Thou shalt be positive and enthusiastic about thy candidate's progress. Celebrate the process more than the achievement, but praise with moderation and evaluate with caution. Remember you are not an assessor.

III. Thou shalt be punctual in thy starting and ending times of meetings.

IV. Thou shalt genuinely and attentively listen to thy candidate, for what they have to say wilt make thee understand them better.

V. Thou shalt document everything!

VI. Thou shalt honor thy candidate's confidentiality, and only share what can be publicly released.

VII. Thou shalt demand and provide honest and ethical behavior, and treat thy candidate as an equal.

VIII. Thou shalt share thy expertise with thy candidate, but allow them to retain ownership in their own work.

IX. Thou shalt always remember to provide snacks whenever possible.

X. Thou shalt provide some measure of celebration when thy candidate mails the box. Honor the process, not merely the victory.

Getting outside help

There will be times when you simply need more help and information than you have available. Below are listed some sources for additional help in your mentoring process. Be discriminating with any information you get outside the *NBPTS* headquarters. Remember—the *NBPTS* alone is the final authority.

Contact *NBPTS* by phone: 1-800-22TEACH

Chat rooms and message boards

OK, this one is controversial. Many will disagree, but I suggest you locate and utilize the online chat and support groups such as the ones in *YAHOO* geared to *NBPTS* certification. These support groups are made up of individuals who are willing to help you at virtually any time of the day or night. There are even some chat rooms devoted specifically to mentors. The insights and suggestions available in these online resources are invaluable.

Yahoo chat rooms regarding the *NBPTS*
http://groups.yahoo.com/

Helpful websites:

These are all a part of the official *National Board* website.

Site Map
http://www.NBPTS.org/sitemap/index.html

Candidate Resource Center
http://www.NBPTS.org/candidates/index.cfm

Ethics
http://www.nbpts.org/pdf/policy_ethical_cand_supp.pdf

NBPTS Candidate Guide
http://www.NBPTS.org/candidates/guide/:

Discussion Groups
http://www.NBPTS.org/events/discus.cfm

NBPTS Standards
http://www.NBPTS.org/standards/index.cfm

NBPTS scoring guides
http://www.NBPTS.org/candidates/scoringguides.cfm

Contact NBPTS
http://www.NBPTS.org/help/index.cfm

Assessment Center help
http://www.NBPTS.org/candidates/acob/4_preptstdy.html

Other helpful sites:

Mentoring
http://www.middleweb.com/mentoring.html

http://www.wizzlewolf.com/mentoring.html#Mentoring%20National%20Board%20Candidates

NBPTS Resources—Florida
http://teacherweb.com/FL/StonemanDouglasHS/FloridaNBPTS-WLOE/h0.stm

Mentor-Candidate Agreement: (Sample)
(Courtesy of Eleanor Joyce, NBCT)

The National Board Certification process is a professional and personal growth opportunity that lends itself to working with other professionals. The mentor is a teacher who has successfully been through the process and/or has extensive knowledge of the process. The candidate is the teacher going through the process. It is important that both parties agree to defined terms and conditions before the relationship begins.

Read the statements in the table below. Initial all the statements agreed upon in the box before the statement, sign and date the agreement. Each party keeps a copy of the agreement.

Mentor's name_____ Candidate's name _____

	Mentor's Responsibilities		Candidate's Responsibilities
	Encourage candidates to call 1-800-22TEACH to receive answers to questions.		Call 1-800-22TEACH to receive answers to questions.
	Be familiar with the standards, the portfolio requirements, and the scoring guide.		**Know and understand** the standards, the portfolio requirements, and the scoring guide.
	Read and review entries, watch videos, offer suggestions though guiding questions. **Will not edit written work.**		Find **two editors,** an educator, and a non-educator to edit spelling, grammar, and readability. Educate the editors on the standards and portfolio requirements Create rubric for editors.
	Offer suggestions on organization of materials		Organize materials in a manner that works for the candidate.
	Answer questions related to the process and not the product		Visit websites and access resources. Find a NBCT in content area and ask for support.
	Offer challenging ideas		Accept the challenge ahead
	Ask probing questions		Listen and ask questions
	Encourage thoughtful reflection		Engage in reflection
	Be available when needed		Listen non-judgmentally
	Listen non-judgmentally		Ask questions
	Help build self-confidence of cohort members		Share fears, concerns, and issues with cohort members
	Maintain confidentiality		Maintain confidentially
	Celebrate the completion of steps in the process		Celebrate the completion of steps in the process
	"I understand that the responsibility of the portfolio and preparation for the assessment center rests with the candidate. I agree to guide the candidate through the process and provide support. I will adhere to the NBPTS Guidelines for Ethical Candidate Support."		"I understand that I am solely responsible for creating the portfolio and preparing for the assessment center. I will seek support and advice from someone certified in my content area in addition to my mentor. Achieving National Board certification is solely my responsibility."

Chapter 5

"Knowledge of Students: the Core of Your Candidates' Content"

(The students, the classroom & the lesson)

The most important element in helping your candidate achieve *National Board Certification* is their knowledge of their students. Every activity described and analyzed throughout the writing process should reflect this as the core of its focus. As mentor, you cannot stress this too much.

Students do not learn in isolation. Learning is holistic. Remind your candidates that 'knowledge of students' includes all of the following, and make sure they evidence in their writing how their students:

- Are able to relate to real-world experience
- Act, react, and the rationale for both
- Reveal their goals and aspirations in life
- Develop physically, mentally, emotionally, and socially as an individual
- Have faced hardships in life, and the effect of such
- Express their interests, talents, and learning styles
- Express interpretive skills regarding issues and events
- Deal with peer interaction, and any concerns regarding the same
- Express their perspective on life and the teacher's lessons
- Express their philosophies, values, and biases in life
- Express their relationships with adults and their community
- Respond to challenges and inquiry
- Evaluate their self-worth, and its effect on learning
- Are affected by their socio-economic background
- Require special needs in particular areas of learning

Suggested activity

Have your candidate choose 3 students, and see how many of the above descriptors they can discuss in detail about each student.

As you well know, the portfolio scores are partially determined by how these descriptors are utilized in the design and implementation of instruction. If your candidate knows this and keeps these factors in mind, they are more likely to address the concerns and goals of the process, and will also be more likely to design appropriate tasks for their students. It should be said as well, that sometimes you might have to help your candidate apply these factors, as they may not be sure what impact they have on classroom instruction. Your job is to make them aware of what they *should* know, and help your candidate recognize and implement strategies which facilitate student success.

The Instructional Context

Before any teacher can implement strategies for student learning, they must identify the instructional context. In helping your candidate identify the instructional context, have them address the following questions:

- ✓ What is the age-range, gender and race ratio of the classroom, and how does this affect a given lesson?

- ✓ What are the students' ranges of reading levels?

- ✓ What are the unique physical features of the classroom which might affect the lesson?

- ✓ How might the needs of the gifted/special needs students be addressed in the lesson?

- ✓ How might students with behavioral needs affect the lesson?

- ✓ Is the candidate choosing students representing different learning styles and challenges?

- ✓ What multicultural issues might contribute/influence the lesson?

- ✓ What differences in the socio-economic status of the classroom make-up might influence the lesson?

- ✓ What student attitudes, groupings or cliques might influence the lesson?

- ✓ What is the maturity level and 'personality' of the class, and how does this affect learning?

- ✓ What previous knowledge or prior lessons will contribute to the lesson?

- ✓ Which students will most likely become 'involved' in the lesson, and how will the reticent learner be addressed?

- ✓ What other professionals will be involved, or present in the classroom?

- ✓ What are the individual strengths and weaknesses of the students with whom you will be working?

- ✓ Is the candidate providing in-depth and relevant information about the students selected for the work samples? That is, information regarding the student not only as a learner, but also as a *person?*

<u>*Suggested activity*</u>

Have your candidate work through this list and relate a possible lesson to the make-up of one of his/her classes. This should give the candidate focus in the choosing of a class.

The featured lessons

Remind your candidate that the teaching featured in *Entries 1-3* must come from different units, different lessons, and different points in time. They cannot use the same students in dual entries. Remind them too, that they should not select merely the brightest students, but rather, the most dependable and cooperative ones. Consider also, students who are motivated, and may evidence the most improvement through the process.

While the candidates themselves will have to choose the lessons which they will use for these entries, you may help them better select the individual *students* to feature, especially in the *Entry 1* writing assignment.

<u>*Suggested activity*</u>

In preparing for Entry 1, discuss with your candidate the following considerations in the selection of students:

- ✓ *What instructional challenges do these students represent?*
- ✓ *What overall goals are represented by the two writing assignments?*
- ✓ *How are such goals a part of your holistic objectives for the unit? For the year?*
- ✓ *How dependable will these students be in completing this process?*
- ✓ *What special needs do either (or both) of these students have?*
- ✓ *How well do these students respond to feedback?*
- ✓ *What room to evidence improvement will these student provide?*
- ✓ *How, through these writing assignments, will these students be able to evidence meaningful connections to writing as a tool for learning?*
- ✓ *How might the backgrounds, values, or interests, of the students affect the content of the writing?*

Chapter 6

"The Writing Process: Fabric of Your Candidate's Success"

(Recognizing and practicing effective writing)

Above all else, how your candidate writes up his/her entries determines success or failure in the certification process. The written entries are all the assessors will have to evaluate. Make sure your candidate's writing is *crisp, clear, and correct*, and that they clearly understand—and can distinguish between—the three types of writing required.

The types of writing the *NBPTS* expects

You must make sure your candidate distinguishes between the three types of writing when composing their written work. One of the leading causes of reduced scoring in the *NBPTS* certification process is a failure to distinguish between these three types of writing, and a failure to *fully* address the requirements evidenced through each type.

As you well know, writing is the heart and soul of the portfolio. Emphasize to your candidate that they write as though they were building a case, and support all statements with concrete evidence At this point let's review the three types of writing for *NBPTS* portfolios.

Descriptive writing

Descriptive writing simply *describes, lists,* or *summarizes*. Descriptive writing answers *what, when, where,* and *how.* It is clear, logical, detailed and precise.

Analytical writing

Analytical or *interpretive* writing involves breaking down, examining, and explaining information. Analytical writing answers the *what's* of descriptive writing with *why's*, *how's*, and *so what's* regarding the lesson's goals, objectives, and effectiveness. It is the thinking behind the teaching.

Reflective writing

Reflective writing answers the questions: 'What did *you learn* from the lesson and student work?' 'What would you *modify* or do differently if you were to do the lesson again?' Remind your candidate to include both positive and negative experiences in their reflective writing.

Essentially the *Written Commentary Section* of each entry follows the same format in which the three types of writing are used. Make sure your candidate understands not only the three types of writing, but also where each is to be used. The following descriptors are referenced from *"Preparing for National Board Certification?":* Some Tips from National Board Certified Teachers by Marian Stallings Cook, Educational Consultant:

- ❏ *Instructional Context* section—Mostly **descriptive** writing is utilized here as questions regarding student numbers and grade levels are addressed. This section is foundational to the *NBPTS* portfolio writing. Make sure your candidate meets every requirement of the *Instructional Context*. Assessors can only evaluate the process if they are given all the required information first.

- ❏ *Planning* section—includes writing that is both **descriptive** (what is taught and learned) and **analytical** ('so what' regarding that teaching and learning). This is where the candidate demonstrates the understanding of standards-based teaching. Here, the important word *evidence* first appears. Emphasize to your candidate that assertions without evidence will not stand critical assessment. Sweeping generalities without evidence are the hallmark of low-scoring entries.

- ❏ <u>Analysis</u> section—This is **analytical** writing with some **reflection**. Here, is the 'dissection' of student learning (analysis), and the implications of that analysis (reflection). The most difficult aspect of your candidate's writing process is in this, and the following section.

- ❏ <u>Reflection</u> section—**Reflective** writing is where your candidate discusses how they feel completed lessons fared, and how future instruction will be impacted. Some **description** (how that instruction might be done) is also included here. This is the 'where do I go from here?' section. Do not allow your candidate to simply retell what they did. This section should be reserved for how the candidate can become a better teacher based on what he/she learned from the lesson.

Suggestions for helping your candidates:

To assist your candidate in the writing process, suggest they:

- Make sure all evidence presented is *clear, consistent, and convincing*
- Use the language of the *NBPTS* Standards
- Not lose their personal voice in their writing
- Use 'for example' in their writing in order to emphasize evidence
- Use direct quotes from student work to assist assessors
- Discuss teaching strategies used, and *why* they were chosen
- Read each other's pieces and provide feedback (in group settings)
- Ask at least 3 other individuals to read their pieces: someone teaching in the subject area, someone teaching out of the subject area, and a professional uninvolved with education.

<u>Suggested activity</u>

Have your candidates read the following Analysis of Student Work excerpts from a social studies portfolio prompt, and identify as many things as they can that distinguish between Scenario 1 (an Inferior Response) and Scenario 2 (an Accomplished Response.).

Instructional goal: "Students will be able to describe the importance of a river system they would like to visit, and relate the importance of that water system to life in any ancient culture."

Scenario 1

In my social studies class, the students were given time to answer the prompt, after which I collected the work. This assignment followed a movie they watched. In Jeremy's work sample I saw some difficulties right off the bat. I knew he (obviously) had not understood the social studies assignment. I was hoping he would be able to relate the assignment to my instructional goals. Jeremy's writing shows me that he still hasn't learned to spell at a high school level, that he needs more practice in learning about the Nile River, and how important river systems are to cultures. I wanted my students to apply their knowledge using personal examples, but Jeremy got totally confused. I gave the assignment again and he showed improvement in this geography lesson. His original difficulty could have been that he's one of my collaborative students, but I don't think so because the rest of the students seemed to get it. As a class we studied the importance of river systems, and I know my students—especially Jeremy—love Egypt, therefore I was not surprised many of them chose to use the Nile. Jeremy didn't seem to be discussing the Nile however, but after I talked to him, I discovered he misunderstood me, and he finally got it!

Scenario 2

As part of our semester-long study of technology in the ancient world, my sophomore students were assigned to answer the given prompt. They were shown a PowerPoint presentation on river systems, and given an hour to complete the assignment, at which time their work was turned in. We had previously created—as a class—a rubric by which the assignment would be graded. Jeremy's work sample exhibited major problems, not the least of which was his grammar and spelling. I learned early in the year from his father that Jeremy has always had difficulty with spelling, but since Jeremy generally does better work than this—recently scoring 92% on an Egyptian essay—I knew something else was wrong. Jeremy is a collaborative student with a severe and identified learning disability, but because of his other successful work, I did not believe this disability explained all of Jeremy's difficulty with this assignment. Jeremy also showed he misunderstood the prompt. For example, in prior lessons, Jeremy expressed his passion for boating and fishing, as well as his love for studying ancient Egypt. Knowing this, my hope was that Jeremy might relate the importance of the Nile River to survival and trade in ancient Egypt. Jeremy did indeed choose the Nile, but as evidenced by his reference to "oak trees", and "the river that flows south into the gulf", I knew Jeremy was not describing the Nile. To be certain, I conferenced with him about what he had described, and realized that he misunderstood me to say "describe the importance of a river you have visited" rather than "describe the importance of a river you'd like to visit". On the revised assignment sheet, Jeremy mentioned cities such as 'Cairo' and 'Memphis', and discussed: "…the papyrus that grows only here…". In addition, through his reference to "means of transport and trade", I also realized that Jeremy had made the connection regarding at least one aspect of the importance of river systems. From these references I knew he now understood the assignment. The mistake had been mine. I will be sure next time to have students restate the assignment for clarity.

Now, have your candidate answer the following specific prompts:

- List several ways the two scenarios differed.
- List several ways the second scenario is a better entry.
- Where was evidence *NBPTS* Standards were addressed?
- In which entry was 'knowledge of students' most effective? How?
- Show the evidence for the three types of *NBPTS* writing in these scenarios.

Chapter 7

"Evidence, Scoring & Assessment: Student Learning & the Standards"

(Helping your candidate know what the assessors will be looking for)

The scoring of the portfolio

At some time during your mentoring tenure, your candidate will bring up the question of how their portfolio will be scored. You need to address this issue with them. As you well know, the rubric against which the entries are measured is valued—and the percentages multiplied—by a number from 4.25 down to 0.75. The higher the number, the more accomplished the work. You should review with your candidate the following writing value levels:

Level 4—Clear, consistent, and convincing evidence is offered. To score at this level, the writing must reflect insightful, logical, in-depth, and appropriate information. Writing must be tightly connected and accurately detailed.

Level 3—Similar to the above, but less-detailed, and/or more loosely constructed, and containing information that is more ambiguous. Writing may be clear, but is not as consistent or convincing.

Level 2—Inaccurate or vague information, illogical or too generalized application. A limited amount of *evidence* is offered.

Level 1—Incomplete entries, or entries with unrelated or inappropriate details. Very unclear, simplistic writing.

Remind your candidate that he/she does not have to score a certain level for any of the entries in order to pass. *It is only the total score that matters.*

It is also important to remind them that a different assessor will score each entry of the portfolio. Each entry should be treated as if it was completely separate in its instructional context.

Since evidence is the heart and soul of the writing process, make sure the evidence presented by your candidate is analyzed, assessed, and evaluated in light of the lesson goals and *NBPTS* Standards.

Level 4 in the rubric should be the goal for your candidates. That being the case, have your candidates measure their writing against the following *NBPTS* Level 4 description, taken from the *NBPTS Middle Childhood/Generalist Standards* instruction guide. (While certification areas differ, your candidate's writing should reflect all or most of these.)

- Recognition of individual learning differences and past experiences
- High, worthwhile, and appropriate goals for student learning
- A variety of assignments for a variety of audiences in building student understanding
- The fostering of student responsibility for his/her own writing development
- Engagement in reflective thinking that demonstrates a clear understanding of past teaching

<u>Suggested activity</u>

If a level 4 exemplar is furnished in your candidate's portfolio, have them read it through several times, circling key words, and explain what 5 things about the piece make it an exemplar.

It bears repeating that the candidate's writing will be assessed on how they present evidence of aligning goals, students, and instruction. As you read your candidate's entries, use the following checklist to assure such alignment has been addressed:

- Do they evidence a broad knowledge of their students?
- Do they present a specific learning goal for each entry?

- Are the goals age-appropriate?
- Do the goals fit into a longer-range objective?
- Do the activities teach or reflect the stated goals?
- Do they evidence strategies to teach the goals?
- Do they address what came before and what will come after the lesson?
- Is this sequence appropriate?
- What technology/multimedia did they use?
- Do these resources provide for individual student differences?
- Does the lesson make connections to real world experience for the students?
- Did they make connections to students' interests and backgrounds?
- Did they assess student work? What were the criteria?
- Were the students made aware of these criteria for assessment?
- Did students have an opportunity to self-assess their work?
- Was feedback given students regarding their progress toward the stated goals?
- Did the lesson make a connection to other subject areas?

<u>*Suggested Activity*</u>

Have your candidate re-read the two scenarios in the previous chapter and note how many items from the above checklist were featured.

Because many candidates are concerned about how their entries will be scored, you should remind your candidate that the scoring process is somewhat complicated, but extremely *fair*. Remind your candidate that no one teacher reads all 10 components of a candidate's performances. According to *"Myths about the NBPTS"*, from the *NBPTS* Resource Center—Florida, "…the performances of first-time candidates in existing certificates are scored by a minimum of 12 practicing classroom teachers and 25% of a candidate's work is double-scored. In addition, due to read-behinds by trainers (who are also practicing classroom teachers) and cases needing adjudication, third reads are often made. All performances submitted by retake candidates are always double-scored. All candidate work submitted for new certificate areas are double-scored in the first year of their administration, which means a minimum of 20 practicing classroom teachers have looked at a candidate's performances in these certificates. In addition, each portfolio entry is scored in a different location of the country, and the same portfolio entry is usually scored by the same group of assessors, which enables *NBPTS* to catch identical cases submitted by two different candidates."

Even a standard deviation (usually between 10-18 points) is figured into the final score to negate any mathematical error. You may also want to tell your candidates:

- Assessors are instructed to identify, record, and evaluate only the evidence provided.

- Assessors are instructed to look for what's right—not what's wrong. They are not 'grading papers'; they are collecting evidence.

- Spelling and grammar are not penalized, and points are not deducted if a name is inadvertently left in, or a margin is slightly askew.

The key to all writing is the *NBPTS* Standards. These standards are extrapolated into the *NBPTS Five Core Propositions*, and are the *only* criteria for measurement used by the assessors. It is not necessary for your candidate to address standards from the state or local school district.

Suggested activity

Have your candidate take their standards document and highlight in different colors the things they do most of the time, things they do some of the time, and things which they feel they need to work on. They might also distinguish in colors:

- *Phrases & concepts that appear repeatedly (these are extremely important)*
- *Anything the standards mention that 'an accomplished teacher' does*
- *Key 'buzzwords' that appear repeatedly (standards-based 'language')*

Finally, have your candidate write down how they might put into practice—or put into practice in a different way—the concepts, accomplished teacher practices, and exemplars, which they highlight.

Chapter 8

"Tips & Reflections on Entries 1-4"

(Carefully examining every aspect of your candidate's portfolio; Sample forms)

This chapter is merely a compilation of general tips, strategies, and activities your candidate should keep in mind throughout the process.

<u>*General tips for getting started*</u>

- Have your candidate make a list of the standards they want to demonstrate in each entry.

- Have your candidate compile a list of the main criteria for each entry.

- Have your candidate brainstorm a list of possible lessons for each entry. (Remind them to consider the standards and criteria.)

- Brainstorm with your candidate to see which lessons best meet the criteria and standards. (Remind them that selected lessons must meet ALL of the requirements/criteria, or they need to select another lesson.)

- Remind your candidate that the most important aspect of choosing students is to evidence student growth.

- Have your candidate provide some form of student assessment, or self-assessment from a student. The ability for students to assess their own strengths, weaknesses, and growth is *extremely* strong evidence.

- Suggest to your candidate that some type of open-ended question be included in Entry 1. Such questions are ideal in providing the students an avenue to express creativity and understanding.

- Encourage your candidate to be unique or creative in at least some part of their portfolio. There is no one right way to teach or compile a portfolio! In fact, many assessors have expressed surprise at how little original material is presented. Have your candidate come up with new and original types of prompts, assessments, activities, or at least a few new slants on old ones.

- The primary reason entries receive low scores is that most candidates fails to answer the entire question completely. **You might have your candidate type in the questions and sub-questions** in order to avoid this pitfall. (These may be removed once the answer is completed.)

- The second most important reason scores are low is that most candidates are not *specific* enough in their writing. Remind your candidate not to use sweeping generalities. (Note the difference between: "Many students understood the concept of immigration," and "I knew Mary understood the concept of immigration when she mentioned the difficulties her family experienced in coming to this country ten years ago.")

- The third most important reason scores are low is that most candidates do not follow directions *accurately*. **Have your candidate highlight their specific instructions, (especially note the verbs!) or read the instructions to you, and explain precisely how they followed them.**

Suggestions for Entry 1

Remind your candidate:

- Samples of student work must show *progression* through the entry.

- They should include comments or feedback (to the student—not the assessor) on student work to show guidance through the process. Comments should relate to more than grammar and spelling. They should be evaluative and meaningful in helping the student understand what needs correction and how he/she needs to change the writing in order to improve it.

- Rubrics are valuable. A rubric or grading sheet shared with the student then used for assessment is an excellent inclusion. Student-created rubrics are valuable also.

- They must evidence give-and-take details between teacher and student.

- If copies (rather than originals) of student work are submitted, color copies should be sent. These will help the assessor distinguish comments from student work.

As your candidate reflects back on the writing samples of the students, have them be sure they discussed in detail the following considerations:

- ✓ How, through these writing assignments, were these students able to evidence meaningful connections to writing as a tool for learning?
- ✓ How does each student's response reflect his or her growth as a writer?
- ✓ How does each student exhibit growth as a writer throughout the drafting process?
- ✓ How does each student evidence learning through the feedback given by the candidate?
- ✓ How successful was the candidate in helping these students develop personal expression through these writing pieces? What evidence is presented to validate this?
- ✓ What would the candidate do differently with these same students next time? Why?

Suggestions for Entries 2-3

The videos provide evidence that assessors use to see how the teacher's plans result in meaningful learning experiences for students. As mentor, you cannot choose the lesson, class, or video entries for submission, but you may help your candidate choose based upon some general considerations.

In assessing your candidate's videos, scorers generally read the written commentary first and watch the video afterward. It is extremely important that the former reflect, explain, and clarify the latter. The scorers will be looking for:

- **Knowledge of Students**—Your candidate's writing should reflect personal knowledge of individual students, not just students as a class. This could include family background, learning style, lesson modification, interrelationship with other students and adults, etc.

- **Meeting Lesson Goals**—That is, how the goals of the lesson are relevant to the standards and the students. Remind your candidate that they must also discuss the 'why' of such relevance as well as how they know such goals are relevant. *Stress specificity!*

- **Did the students 'get it'?**—And how did your candidate know the students understood the lesson (or not)? Stress the use of questioning for assessment during the taping, as well analysis of student discussion which was evidenced.

- **Student engagement**—as revealed through group discussion, relevant comments, answered questions, etc. Remind your candidate to include as many students as possible in the video.

What the *NBPTS* wants to see—considerations regarding videotapes:

- Are diversity and respect addressed? How?

- Are the students *reasoning, discussing,* and *concluding? What is the evidence?*

- Is the candidate handling the *anticipated,* the *expected,* and the *unexpected* incidents?

- Is there *interaction* (verbal and nonverbal) between students, and teacher/students in the learning process?

- Were the room and seating arrangements appropriate for the lesson?

- Is the discourse *relevant to* the lesson, and does it help students achieve instructional goals?

- Can all students be heard and faces seen?

- Were differentiated learning goals set for individual students, and were such goals met in the video? What is the evidence?

- Were the reluctant learners encouraged? How is this evidenced?

- Were students quoted in the writing to emphasize importance and/or to clarify any possibility they were not heard accurately?

- Was risk-taking promoted? What is the evidence?

- What learning opportunities did the candidate take advantage of, and/or miss, in the video. What is the evidence? What would they do next time?

- Did any unanticipated 'teachable moments' occur, and how were they handled? What did the candidate learn from them?

- Was student learning clearly evidenced? How?

- Were multiple intelligences being addressed?

- Did students see relevance in the lesson? How could this be seen?

- Did the students evidence a link to prior learning and/or personal experience in the lesson? Where in the video?

- Was there evidence of assessment—especially student assessment—in the video?

- Were students redirected when necessary?

- Were students challenged through high level questioning?

- Were any misconceptions addressed adequately?

- Does the video demonstrate a high level of rapport and mutual respect between teacher and students? How is this evidenced?

- Does the teacher demonstrate such a connection through use of students' names, feedback, eye contact, and movement?

- Does the teacher show enthusiasm and energy for the topic and for the students?

- Does the teacher provide for student reflection and consideration during the video?

- Does the teacher exhibit active listening skills toward the students?

Suggested Activity

Have your candidate share their videos with a colleague or friend. Get their input on what worked and what didn't. When they have narrowed their best videos down to two or three, have them watch each one 4 times.

- ✓ *Have them watch each once by themselves. Have them take notes on the positives and negatives of each session.*

- ✓ *Have them watch each once with their students, note all insightful comments made, and have your candidate include these in their writing analysis and reflection.*

- ✓ *Have them watch each once with a friend or colleague, and solicit their input.*

✓ Have them watch each once silently—*volume turned off*. Then have them analyze and reflect in their writing what they learned from all 4 viewings.

A final note about using tapes. Remind your candidate to use a high quality tape, and black out (by leaving the camera cap on) the first two minutes of the tape. Assessors begin when the video starts, and the first part of videotapes are notorious for rough quality.

Suggestions for Entry 4: Documented Accomplishments

The Documented Accomplishments Entry is the same for all areas. **"Less is more in Entry 4"** is one of the finest suggestions to offer your candidate here. That is, your candidate will likely be more successful including *fewer* accomplishments with more cogent detail than a large number of accomplishments intended to impress. Also, remind your candidate that the focus here is on:

- Parent interaction and family involvement (within the last year)
- Community involvement (within the last year)
- Professional growth—teacher as learner, leader, collaborator (within the last 5 years)

The evidence must clear, convincing, and consistent, and be student-learning centered. The candidate should not mention what they cannot prove.

Suggested activity

When your candidate has gathered artifacts to be considered as Documented Accomplishments, have them write and explain answers to the following:

- ✓ "I chose this as a Documented Accomplishment because—"
- ✓ "This accomplishment addresses the standard—"
- ✓ "This accomplishment relates to my portfolio instructions in that—"
- ✓ "This is a valid 'accomplishment' because—"
- ✓ "This accomplishment contributed to my students' learning by—"
- ✓ "I know all three areas of this entry are covered because—"
- ✓ "The most student-centered aspect of this accomplishment is—"

It is important to remind your candidate to keep their *personal accomplishments* discussion to a minimum. As Richard Wedig, *NBCT*, notes: "'Teacher of the Year' accolades, advanced degrees, extracurricular activity sponsorship, and personal travel are not in themselves, the best choices for entries." In addition, some entries may overlap. That is, they may evidence what the candidate does as a learner and a collaborator, or how they involve parents as a part of the community. If your candidate uses dual entries, be sure they explain the particular *focus*.

Do not allow your candidate to get too stressed out about this entry. Generally, Entry 4 is the most troublesome to organize. The key is to remind them to focus on entries that directly 'touch the students' first. That is, entries which best evidence how the candidate recognized and understood individual students' strengths, weaknesses and needs. Such entries will always carry more weight.

Below are questions to ask your candidate as they prepare Entry 4:

- ✓ What is the significance and impact of this accomplishment? (Why is it important?)
- ✓ Did this accomplishment occur in the last 5 years?
- ✓ Does the accomplishment reflect the *NBPTS* Standards?
- ✓ How does the accomplishment impact your students, and influence student learning, and how can these outcomes—with specific examples—be demonstrated—in the writing?
- ✓ How do you know this accomplishment was successful in its impact on student learning? Is there a clear connection in the writing?
- ✓ Does this accomplishment reflect how you *recognized* and *met* a student need? (It is important for the teacher to meet the student needs—not just recognize them!)
- ✓ Do you have an accomplishment for each area of Entry 4?
- ✓ Is there documentation that your work with parents occurred this year?
- ✓ Does interaction with parents include two-way communication?
- ✓ Are there any accomplishments which might better be clustered and written about as one accomplishment?
- ✓ Does the accomplishment reflect how you are going 'above and beyond' what is expected of every teacher, or is it routine and required?

- ✓ Do accomplishments indicate your growth in professional development, and/or improvement in the teaching practice?
- ✓ Do you reflect upon the patterns in your accomplishments, and how your future as a teacher might be impacted?
- ✓ Does your accomplishment contribute to the advancement of your colleagues and/or the education profession in general? How?

Suggestions for getting started on Entry 4

- ❑ Brainstorm with your candidate everything they have done professionally over the past few years. Have them go through their files, old calendars, professional growth plans, and especially planning books.

- ❑ Brainstorm with your candidate how they have involved parents and their community in their teaching. Include everything. (This list can be revised later.)

- ❑ Have your candidate reflect on which activities have had the most impact on student learning in general, as well as individual student learning, in their class, this year. Remind them that *student learning* includes more than school activity. It is physical, emotional, behavioral, and social learning also! It is important to remind your candidate that different students are impacted in different ways. Very seldom is an entire class 'impacted' in the same way. The more your candidate can discuss diverse impacts on individual students, the more effective will be the entry. For example, "What modifications in instructions and/or assessment impacted Susie's learning?"

- ❑ With your candidate, re-read the specific standards for Entry 4. Have them highlight or note the key phrases and important ideas. Compare how their activities reflect these standards.

Accomplishments might include (but are not restricted to):

- ❑ a signed agenda book

- ❑ a student monitoring contract

- online, teacher-created web pages (such as *Schoolnotes.com*) to keep students and parents continually informed, or a web page of student helps

- a communication log—a *series* of parent contacts through phone logs, and/or emails regarding a particular student. Remind your candidate that the contact does not have to be by phone or email only. It can include even casual chats at soccer games, at Sears, etc., but the majority should be ongoing, back-and-forth contact all year

- a newspaper article about the candidate with quotes from former students

- peer coaching contracts

- online student reviews (of books or films) that evidence student accomplishment (*Amazon.com* welcomes these)

- student work denoting use of a new skill

- innovative use of technology benefiting students or colleagues

- a copy of improved state test scores in the candidate's area of teaching

- at least one Verification Form (The Verification Form is used to validate an accomplishment—*and* its impact on student learning, for which there is no tangible artifact.) Be sure what is written on the Verification Form matches what is explained in the entry, and that the person verifying states clearly how the accomplishment impacted student learning

- parent letters extolling a learning strategy that was especially successful

- a letter from an esteemed colleague or notable educator or community person

- letters or articles written for professional journals

- mentoring, or working as a peer teacher

- ❏ a personal, reflective journal

- ❏ having community-based, non-profit organizations (such as Junior Achievement, Rotary Clubs, etc.) come and work with students for an extended period

- ❏ leadership roles in professional organizations

- ❏ student-led conferences where students help students by sharing achievement strategies

- ❏ community photos

- ❏ documented evidence of the candidate's attendance or presentation at a conference or workshop

- ❏ leadership in a staff development endeavor

- ❏ newsletters

- ❏ parent surveys and questionnaires—these are especially good. The more the parent is willing to put, the better

- ❏ especially poignant student letters

- ❏ student teaching assignments

Whatever your candidate chooses to include, make sure their evidence is clear, convincing, and consistent, is student-centered in the writing, and that it resulted in—or was likely to result in—student learning.

Note the following sample worksheets:

Entry 1: *Student Writing* Matrix (Sample)

	Student 1	Student 2
How did this student *evidence growth* throughout the drafting and revising process?		
How did this student's writing *meet the goals* I set for them?		
How did my feedback to this student *evidence my knowledge of their unique needs, background, and interests?*		
How did my feedback to the student *show guidance?*		
How did this student's implementation of my feedback *evidence student growth* in the writing process?		
How did I assess student work throughout the writing process and how did assessment *contribute to student learning?*		

Entry 2 & 3: *Videos* Evidence Worksheet (Sample)

Is accomplished teacher behavior evidenced through:	What is the Evidence?
Planning with *goals* in mind?	
Setting high *expectations*?	
Questioning techniques?	
Appropriate *'wait' time*?	
Student *involvement* in learning?	
Addressing *multiple intelligences*?	
Utilizing *multiple resources*?	
Cross-curricular connections?	
Real world connections?	
Prior learning connections?	
Adjustments for *teachable moments*?	
Accommodations for specific student needs: *Special needs*, etc.?	
'Safe' environment atmosphere?	
Active engagement by the students?	
Active listening by students/teachers?	
Students *interacting with teacher*?	
Students *interacting with peers*?	
Addressing the *NBPTS Standards*?	

Entry 4: *Documented Accomplishments* Matrix (Sample)

Category	Activity	Significance	Impact on Student Learning	Documentation
What accomplishments can <u>best</u> evidence:	*What activity in your teaching context will best evidence student learning?*	*How does this activity go beyond what is routine for the average teacher and what was its effect on the holistic learning environment?*	*How do you know this accomplishment resulted in student learning? Be specific.*	*What documentation can you furnish to evidence your participation or involvement in this accomplishment or activity?*
How you worked with *parents, other family members, and the community* where your students live.				
How you served as a *leader, collaborator,* and/or professional development provider.				
How you grew and *progressed as a learner* in the professional development process.				

Chapter 9

"Mentoring the Advanced Candidate: Achieving Success the Next time Through"

(Special Considerations)

Candidates who do not certify the first time through may be referred to as 'bankers', or better, as 'advanced candidates'. Advanced candidates should be encouraged to complete the certification process. They have three opportunities to pass. Nevertheless, as you mentor such candidates, realize they have unique needs you must be aware of. In not certifying the first year of candidacy, they have experienced disappointment, embarrassment, and disbelief, which may be hard for you to understand if you passed on the first try.

Initially, the advanced candidate may have felt such anger and frustration that they wanted to quit the process altogether. You must remember—especially with the advanced candidate—that how you communicate with them greatly impacts their disposition in retrying the process. It is up to you to remind them that their initial scores may have been more a reflection on how they *wrote* than on how they *teach*. The assessors do not know them. Remind them too, that the process does not measure the daily influence they have on hundreds of young lives.

There could be many reasons why the advanced candidate did not reach the required 275 points. Perhaps family situations kept them from giving their best effort. Maybe they did not give the certification process enough time, or it could be they did not fully distinguish the types of required writing. According to Yvonne Woodward, NBCT, who has specialized in working with advanced candidates in KY, not allowing enough time for completing the process often appears to be the primary factor in low-scoring portfolios. As mentor, help your candidate develop a timeline, be sure they stick to it, and then check with them routinely to be sure they are on target. If they get behind, it is important that they catch up as soon as possible.

As you analyze previous scores with your candidate, discuss what made the highest scoring area good, and what made the lowest scoring area not as good. Above all, remind your candidate the *NBPTS* certification is a three-year process. Many candidates do not embrace that concept when applying. If candidates understand from the beginning that this may take three years, advanced candidacy is less traumatic. Above all, remind your candidate that when they certify, it will make no difference whether it was on the first, second, or third try. All that will matter is that they are a National Board Certified teacher!

While many of the following tips may be applicable to all candidates, most are of particular concern when working with the advanced candidate:

- Lend an understanding ear, and realize their self-esteem has been dealt a blow. Allow the advanced candidate to vent their frustrations. They do go through a 'grieving' process. Different personalities deal with advanced candidacy differently—some will be bitter, angry, depressed, frustrated, etc. They must vent these frustrations so they can move on and complete certification.

- Be a good listener as to why they think they did not certify, and redirect them toward improvement. Discuss reasons, not excuses.

- Assure them of their accomplished teaching.

- Remind them that they may have different submission schedules and deadlines than first time candidates.

- Help them decide on *what* to retake. The retake entries must be new, or they will not be scored. Retake entries will be compared to the original entries. Within the following 24-months, advanced candidates may retake any entry or combination of entries, which scored <u>less</u> than 2.75. Such entries are generally marked with an "*" on the score report. (Help advanced candidates analyze their highest scoring entry, and why it scored so well. Also, examine the lowest scoring entry and analyze why it scored low in light of the Scoring Guide. It is important to remind your advanced candidates that retake scores REPLACE the original scores—even if they are lower.) If the advanced candidate plans on retaking more than 5-6 entries, you might suggest that they repeat the certification process from the beginning. It becomes more cost effective at this point, and all banked scores are erased. Advanced candidates are then considered to be 'new' candidates.

- Remind them that if their assignment has changed or they are no longer in a classroom setting, they will need to 'borrow' a class in order to fulfill the original portfolio requirements.

- Welcome input from their experiences. Utilize these as valued helps, which will benefit others regarding pitfalls to avoid along the way.

- Give advanced candidates particular attention regarding a timeline and time management. Very often, this is a primary reason for not certifying.

- Remind them that retake portfolios generally pass more than 60% of the time.

- Remind them that assessors do not know previous scores.

- Strongly encourage them to do a completely new unit—nothing remotely related to original entry—the second time through. This will contribute to the 'fresh start' atmosphere advanced candidates need. In addition, they do not want to risk the work being perceived as an edit/revision. (Some things such as contextual information, documentation for accomplishments prior to the current year, etc., may not change. However, candidates must submit completely new descriptions, reflections, and work with students' families and the community, for Entry 4.)

Chapter 10

"Packing the Box & the Assessment Center: Final Considerations"

(Tying up all the loose ends)

In wrapping up our discussion of mentorship, let's discuss some final ways you can help your candidate when the time comes to mail in the box, and/or prepare for the Assessment Center.

Suggested activity

When your candidate has completed the process, celebrate the achievement—perhaps with a gift certificate, flowers, etc. It is important to acknowledge the hard work they have put in.

Here are some final checks regarding the packing of the box:

- ❑ Did they follow the *NBPTS* rules about student names, barcode ID numbers, fonts, margins, pagination, etc.?

- ❑ Did they enlarge (200%) their photo ID and put it on the correct form?

- ❑ Did they include their classroom layout?

- ❑ Did they include all required forms including attestation, Contextual Information and Candidate Final Inventory sheets? Remember—they do not have to submit Adult and Student Release forms, but they must get them signed anyway, and should file them.

- ☐ Did they make the appropriate distinction in their writing between *analyzation, description, & reflection?*

- ☐ Did they make sure their *ID number, date,* and *signature* is on everything applicable?

- ☐ Did they punch out the tabs on the videotapes, rewind them, and put on the *correct* label?

- ☐ Did they pack videos in plastic cases for protection in transport?

- ☐ Did they check the Candidate Final Inventory for each entry?

- ☐ Did they check student work samples against the description in the written commentary to make sure they referred to the correct student?

- ☐ Did they omit last names and school locale references?

- ☐ Did they put their candidate ID barcode on each entry coversheet, envelope, and on the portfolio box?

- ☐ Did they make final copies of everything—student work, videotapes, computer disks, entries, etc.? (Remind them to make a duplicate copy of their portfolio when it is completed, since they do not get their portfolio back when the process is over.)

- ☐ Did they spell-check everything several times using different formats, such as the 'standard', 'casual', 'formal', etc., spell-check options?

- ☐ Did they answer all parts of every question?

- ☐ Did they make sure all videos could be seen and heard sufficiently?

- ☐ Did they document student work samples with identifiers ("Student A", "Student B")?

- ❏ Did they double-check to be sure they referred to the correct student in the writing description and analysis?

- ❏ Did they pack the box securely, and with filling material?

The Assessment Center

Before they go to the Assessment Center, remind your candidates to read the Scoring Guide rubrics for identifiers at each performance level. In preparation for the Assessment Center, encourage your candidates to:

- o Become familiar with Assessment Center Orientation Booklet.

- o Consult outside resources relevant to the content area being assessed (e.g., study guides, articles, periodicals, websites, etc.).

- o Arrive about 30 minutes early to become acclimated.

- o Remember to take their *Authorization to Test* (ATT) verification, two valid forms of identification, and sheet of barcode labels.

- o Make sure in their writing, the key ideas are cited before they worry about appearances and details. (Have them refer back to the writing rubric in Chapter7.)

- o Write *clearly* and *concisely!* Remind them also that they will be evaluated on content, not fluency.

- o Be sure they read and answer the question *carefully* and *completely*, and to answer *all parts* of the question! (To leave out any part is to suffer a substantial reduction in score.)

- o Skip introductions and conclusions. Get to the point, maximize the point and move on.

- o Include any factual and or statistical detail they know to be true and accurate. (Numbers and facts lend an air of authority to the writing.)

- Address the standards in their writing. It is not enough to just list without explanation. Remind them to emphasize learning styles, multiple intelligences, etc.

- Formulate and utilize *cause and effect* information where they are able. (This exemplifies higher-level reasoning skills.)

- Cite *examples* where they are able. (Illustrated evidence is *strong* evidence.)

- Be dogmatic in their opinions. (They should not say, *"I think"*, or *"it is possible."* These weaken the discussion.)

Bibliography and References

Much helpful information was collected from the *National Board Certification Candidate Resource Center.*

<u>Other source material includes</u>:

Bacal, Robert. *"The Role of the Facilitator—Understanding What Facilitators Really DO!",* Work911/Bacal & Associates Business & Management Supersite. (Undated).

Bacon, Ann; Parks, Jerry L. *"Great Tips for Packing the Box!"* (Handout; undated)

Cook, Marian Stallings, Educational Consultant. *"Preparing for National Board Certification?":* Some Tips from National Board Certified Teachers; NEA handout. 2003.

Costa, A., & Garmston, R. *"Cognitive Coaching: Mediating Growth Toward Holonomy."* 1988.

Daines, J., Daines, C., & Graham, B. *"Adult Learning, Adult Teaching",* University of Nottingham. 1993.

Einhorn, Carole. *"Enhanced Architecture of Accomplished Teaching",* National Board Resource Center, Illinois State University. 2002.

Fletcher, Louise. *"National Board Tips"* (Compilation; undated).

Gaddis, Lynn; Director of the National Board Resource Center. *"Strategies for Groups to View Videotapes.* 2002.

Goodland, John. *"Principles of Adult Learning"*; Best Practices Resources (Undated).

Lieb, Stephen. Senior Technical Writer, Arizona Dept. Of Health Services *"Principles of Adult Learning"; VISION.* 1991.

Parks, Jerry L. *"So, You Want to Become a National Board Certified Teacher?"* Weekly Reader Press. 2004.

Paul, Richard. *Critical Thinking: How to Prepare Students for a Rapidly Changing World.* 1993.

Role of Facilitators, Chicago Public Schools Facilitator's Resource Guide. (Undated).

Slattery, N.L. *"Practical Tips for Getting Started With Entry 4".* 2003.

The National Board for Professional Teaching Standards, Appropriate Mentoring Practices: "Ethical Standards"

Wedig, Richard. *"Getting Started on Your Portfolio: Entry 4"* (Unpublished).

Myths about the NBPTS, NBPTS Resource Center—Florida

The National Board for Professional Teaching Standards, Standards for Accomplished Middle Childhood/Generalist Teachers

Tips on Videotaping, Chicago Public Schools Facilitator's Resource Guide

(Answers: 1:no. 2:no. 3:yes. 4:yes. 5:yes. 6:no. 7:yes. 8:no. 9:no. 10:no. 11:no. 12:no. 13:no. 14:yes. 15:yes. 16:yes. 17:no. 18:no. 19:yes!, 20:no. 21:no. 22:yes. 23:no. 24:yes. 25:yes. 26:yes. 27:yes. 28:no. 29:no. 30:no.)

About the Author

Jerry Parks earned B.S., M.A., & Ed.S degrees in education from Eastern Kentucky University, and completed additional graduate work at the University of Kentucky. He became a *National Board Certified Teacher* in 2002, and has received numerous "Teacher of the Year" honors at the local, state, and national level. He is a regular speaker at *National Middle School Association* conferences, and is currently department chairperson and instructor of social studies at Georgetown Middle School in Georgetown, Kentucky.

Dr. Parks is also author of four other books. *"So, You Want to Become a National Board Certified Teacher?"* is a handbook for new *NBPTS* candidates. *"With Joseph in the University of Adversity: The Mizraim Principles"* is based on principles from the life of Joseph the Hebrew in the Old Testament. *"Dragons, Grasshoppers & Frogs!"* is a commentary for teenagers on the Book of Revelation. *"Teacher Under Construction: Things I Wish I'd Known"*, is a handbook to help new middle school teachers in their first year of teaching.

Jerry is currently a mentor, and a Regional Coordinator for the *National Board for Professional Teaching Standards* in the state of Kentucky.

978-0-595-40483-4
0-595-40483-9

Printed in the United States
58428LVS00005B/281